MW00986341

Emergency Preparedness for Mobilehome Communities

A Neighborhood Disaster Survival Guide

Virginia S. Nicols

Dentrovisi, Inc.

Irvine, California

Dentrovisi, Incorporated
4790 Irvine Blvd. Suite 105
Irvine, CA 92620

Book Layout © 2017 BookDesignTemplates.com

Emergency Preparedness for Mobilehome Communities. – Virginia S. Nicols, 1st ed.

ISBN 978-1-9805947-5-8

To be clear . . .

This is not a Plan. It is a guide to help you PRE-PARE and execute your own plan, one tailored to your community's needs.

Every mobilehome community is unique, so while this guide may provide templates, they are not rigid. Rather, you'll get suggestions and options.

You are encouraged to work directly with your community's First Responders whether or not they support an active CERT training activity.

You also acknowledge that circumstances and laws are likely to change over time and will differ from community to community. It is your responsibility to adjust your plan appropriately.

The purpose of the guide is to educate, and not to provide you with any legal, accounting, or other form of business advice. We do not warrant that information contained in this report is fully complete and we shall not be responsible for any errors, omissions, or contradictory information. You and your team bear the responsibility to verify its contents and to make sure that your activities conform to your local needs and laws.

Finally, we can give no guarantee with this guide. Emergencies by their very definition are unexpected and unknown. What we do know, though, is that whatever preparations you make and whatever planning you do gives you a better chance of keeping that emergency from becoming a disaster.

Dedication

This book is dedicated to the committed people of my own southern California neighborhood who have kept on keeping on year after year, with the interests of their neighbors at heart.

Working together is a pleasure. Working together for **others** is inspiring.

I owe these books to your steadfastness.

Virginia Nicols

Why I wrote this book

My partner Joe Krueger and I had been introduced to the amenities of mobilehome living in the late 90s, so when our family in Southern California wanted us nearer the grandchildren, we started our housing search with the nearest mobilehome parks.

We found a great deal in a unique park. And because we had spent the previous 20 years as consultants, living in towns on both coasts, dodging hurricanes and twisters, we were ready to put down some roots.

We soon discovered some things about our new community that made us uneasy:

- This is earthquake country. The famous San Andreas Fault, 30 years overdue for "the big one," runs right by our community. We already had personal experience in the San

Francisco quake of 1989 and knew what could happen.

- The older homes in our community were particularly vulnerable – and most of our neighbors were ill-prepared for a quake or for any other big emergency.
- No real plan was in place to raise awareness or standards.

As luck would have it, during the very first year in our new home, our city began putting on Community Emergency Response Team training. We had the time and the interest and signed up for the 8-week course.

CERT is what kicked everything off!

Of course, in the 90's we had designed and implemented a massive advertising and marketing campaign on Disaster Recovery services for a major utility. In putting that campaign together for 11 western states we had done some real spadework. We interviewed many businesses, attended a national Disaster Recovery conference, etc. The campaign was a major organizational challenge, and very rewarding.

(The campaign was one of our most successful, by the way. It ultimately pulled a 90% response from the headquarters of major corporations and added to our collection of national marketing awards! The secret to the campaign's success was Joe's experience in military intelligence, teaching senior military officers how to protect their military installations from natural disasters and civil disturbances. This required organizational skills very different from fighting wars!)

Pulling together volunteers in a community – especially one largely populated by senior citizens – is also a distinct organizational challenge. We saw that the CERT program was going to be a major part of the solution for our community!

Once CERT was available . . .

On September 11, 2001 it became more than a luxury for private citizens to be educated and prepared to deal with disasters, man-made as well as natural.

Knowing we couldn't build a neighborhood "program" by ourselves, we began encouraging our neighbors to take the CERT course.

Once a number were CERT trained they became the nucleus of a team. Interest continued to grow, and we now have almost three dozen CERT graduates in our neighborhood! These people have become leaders, sustaining a group that has grown at times to be as large as 100 volunteers!

All along the way we have used CERT materials as the inspiration for our community activities. We have had to make some creative adjustments, of course. First, to accommodate senior citizen capabilities and budgets. Second, to include the diverse backgrounds of our neighbors. Third, to take advantage of the particular skills and interests of some of our group members. (Pets, for example, are a big deal for our neighborhood. We come back again and again to how to protect them in an emergency.)

Also along the way we presented a proposal to our Homeowners' Association, requesting funds so we could invest in supplies. Over the years we have purchased two-way radios, first aid supplies and, yes, we even have a stock of body bags.

Our neighborhood team responded.

Members of our team have responded to five major gas leaks and three fires in the community, helping save people and property until First Responders could take over. As a result, we have received awards from the city and ten of our people have been recognized by the Chief of Police with personal citations.

The most important recognition of all, however, is the knowledge that we are all better prepared to take care of ourselves in the face of a wide variety of disasters.

This guide is the result of our community's real life experience over more than a dozen years in building a team and a plan. We update the book regularly to respond to new preparedness realities.

The book documents everyday actions we have taken and that you can take. We believe they will enhance your personal safety and help build a neighborhood team you can count on.

Please note the stories labeled "*Real Life*." They are specific examples of some of the hard lessons we've learned. Read those with particular care!

Virginia Nicols

P.S. I welcome your comments and questions. You will find our email and phone number at our website, https://emergencyplanguide.org

P.P.S. Even before you jump into the pages of this book, consider heading right now to our website to sign up for our weekly Advisories. Advisories are free, and they address many different aspects of emergency preparedness with the goal of raising awareness and imparting valuable know-how. Don't miss a single one!

CONTENTS

Survival Planning for Mobilehome and Manufactured Home Communities

Whether you go through a natural or a man-made disaster, the reality after the event is pretty much the same.

Suddenly you are deprived of nearly everything you've become accustomed to.

Just think of what is affected when something simple happens, like the electricity going out . . .

No lights
No cooking
No bottle warmer
No coffee maker
No TV
No phone

No refrigeration
No freezer
No ice
No dishwasher
No clothes washer

. . . and the list goes on.

You won't have access to the ATM for cash. With no electricity for gas pumps, refrigeration or electronic door openers, stores and gas stations won't have the ability to sell to you. Banks and stores will be closed.

The pharmacy will have the same problems – no ability to check records, no cash register to take payments. Your pharmacy will be closed.

You'll find it difficult and probably impossible to get needed medications.

If the water goes out, too, just going to the bathroom will be a major problem.

The water system most likely depends on electricity. You will likely have a problem with running water and sewer. Think about how many times a day you go to the bathroom and multiply that by the number of people in your household and the total of all residents in your park!

You won't have long to wait before human waste becomes a major health issue for you and other residents.

If you haven't seen the value in planning until now, or if you find yourself procrastinating because you just don't know how to begin, we hope this guide will get you started.

We've tried to fill it with ways to take sensible and mostly inexpensive steps to prepare yourself and your neighbors to overcome or at least manage through these inconveniences.

Unique Challenges and Opportunities for Mobilehome Dwellers

Have you done much research about emergency preparedness online?

If so, you probably found that most everything is aimed at people living in a single family home, often in a rural setting.

Living in an urban or suburban multi-unit mobilehome or manufactured home community is simply different.

It has advantages and some special challenges. That's why we felt obliged to write this!

KNOW THESE VOCAB DISTINCTIONS

Before we jump in more deeply, let's get some language straight. (This section may apply more to people reading the book who don't actually LIVE in a mobile or manufactured home.) There are definitely some distinctions to be made between trailers, mobilehomes, and manufactured homes.

Here's how we use the words in Emergency Preparedness for Mobilehome Communities:

Trailer – In its basic form, a trailer is platform or box with wheels that is pulled behind a truck or car and used to transport things. Some trailers are built as traveling homes, with beds, a kitchen and bathroom, etc. People park their trailers permanently or temporarily in recreation areas or in trailer parks. The important thing about trailers is that they are meant to be moved on regular roads towed by regular passenger cars or trucks.

Mobilehome (spelled as one word or two) – As trailers got bigger, they became more home and less mobile. Mobilehomes are towed into place, usually by a semi truck, set up on their site (often with a permanent foundation), and are not expected to be moved again (although they could be). Typical mobilehomes are "singlewide" – a 10 foot or 12 foot wide section, moved in one piece – or "doublewide," two sections moved separately and joined permanently on the site. Doublewides are thus typically 20 to 24 feet across. Mobilehomes vary in length from 20 to as much as 90 feet per section.

Manufactured home – In 1976 prefabricated homes came under the jurisdiction of the federal government. Assembled in factories under strict supervision, they follow more traditional home building processes and building codes. These homes are also delivered to their final location by specialty trucks. While the overall shape of the home is still roughly a large rectangular box, the footprint may include cutouts or extensions. The interior varies considerably as to number and layout of rooms, ceiling height, amenities like fireplaces, porches, skylights, etc. From both inside and out, a manufactured home may be indistinguishable from a traditional stick-built home.

In my experience, manufactured home owners may refer to their homes as "mobilehomes," but mobilehome and manufactured home owners will NEVER call their home a "trailer," because of the unfortunate association with the expression "trailer trash."

Thanks for knowing and respecting these vocabulary distinctions!

PREPAREDNESS CHALLENGES PECULIAR TO MOBILEHOMES

Finding space to store your emergency supplies in a mobilehome takes creativity! Your shed may offer some options. If your home is a singlewide, you will have additional restrictions on space for storage.

If your home is old, or you don't own it, you won't be able to do any major remodeling as a protection against weather or other threats. Again, keep reading for some easy-to-manage improvements.

In older units, your only access to the outside may be limited to doors on either side of the home, limiting escape routes. Newer units offer escape through windows, too.

Depending on the type of park you live in, your neighbors may be elderly or transient and change often, making it challenging to build any stable emergency "teams."

Many older parks were constructed in outlying areas, along railroad rights of way. Over the years these campuses have undergone various development and zoning changes. It's important to know where your community stands in this regard.

AND, SOME IMPORTANT ADVANTAGES.

As you will see, our philosophy is:

"Lives will be saved or lost in the first few minutes following a disaster – and the people who will be there first and able to make a difference are your neighbors."

So here are some things to consider regarding neighbors:

In a family park, you may have an "instant," capable community to work with. Of course, many residents will be at work during the day. Residents in a senior community, by comparison, may have physical limitations but most of them will likely be at home when an emergency arises.

Everyone will have a pretty good idea of what to expect in an emergency because they live in similar circumstances.

A congenial group of neighbors could invest as a group in important emergency equipment that a single person or a single family would not be able to manage.

As a group, you and your neighbors may be able to attract speakers, grant money and other resources that would not be possible for any of you on your own.

The bottom line: survival will be a community project. Like it or not, you and other residents of the park are in this together.

First, of course, people are responsible for themselves. That's what **Part One** of the Guide focuses on. (And let me say right at the outset, getting people to take this responsibility is the most frustrating aspect of the whole effort!)

Next, people need to acquire more survival skills – and that's **Part Two**.

The meat of the Guide really begins to appear with **Part Three** – helping you build a Plan that pulls everything and everybody together.

It's no exaggeration to say that your lives may depend on each other's skills, commitment and advance preparations.

How well you cooperate in preparing yourselves now may determine who lives and who dies if (or when) disaster strikes.

Part One: Your Personal Safety

The "list" of what emergency supplies you should have can or would want can be endless, depending on the size of your family, the type of home you live in, where you live, your budget, etc.

After 15 years we have come up with a simplified list to get you started: eight categories for personal safety and security.

I hope you find them familiar; maybe you've already followed up on some or most of them. As you read, if you see you've missed an item or two, we've included a page at the end of each chapter for your notes.

If these suggestions make sense, consider sharing the list not only with your immediate neighbors but also with park management, property owner or

homeowners' association. Ask them to
distribute the list to all residents.

Don't expect to deal with all eight of
these areas, all at once, in just a couple of
days!

Slow and steady is a lot easier. For
example, you may want to work on one
area per week. If you have an Association,
you could use the list as the agenda for a
weekly announcement or even a weekly
meeting.

We end up inviting guest speakers on
the various topics, and doing a lot of
"show and tell" that involves neighbors.
Anything to keep the momentum going!

In any event, the more prepared you
AND your neighbors are, the easier and
safer it's going to be for all of you in the
face of a real emergency.

But wait, I'll bet you have questions
like these!

"WHAT ABOUT THE AUTHORITIES?"

When asked, "Who will come to help
you in an emergency?" many people
automatically answer, "Well, isn't that the
job of the Red Cross?"

You wish!

Keep in mind that fire, rescue and police will be overwhelmed by a large-scale emergency. It may be several hours or even several days before they arrive with assistance. Relief organizations like the Red Cross or FEMA won't be coming in until AFTER the First Responders have been able to get there.

Remember Hurricane Sandy? Have you seen the video of the woman angrily yelling into the news camera, "We're starving here and it's been three days and we haven't seen ANYone from the government!" In a big emergency, that will be the reality.

(More recent news from Puerto Rico is far worse. You can find loads of examples of where "the authorities" were absent.)

"AND WHAT ABOUT OUR PROPERTY MANAGERS?"

Unfortunately, the people managing your park are probably contractually limited to protecting it – not you. In fact, you may find out that your property managers are specifically prohibited from taking any responsibility for residents! (If your park is managed by a caring and conscientious owner, things may be different. More on park owners later.)

So what it boils down to is . . .

It's up to you.

The work you put in on your own is what will determine how well and how comfortably you get through it all.

What follows are basic recommendations. Where you see an asterisk, we make a specific recommendation in the list of supplies in the Appendix. You'll find other resources there too, each with its own list.

Getting yourself and your family prepared is a reasonably straightforward process – it just takes time!

Consider these eight steps as "starters" and add to them as necessary. We've included a section at the end of this chapter for NOTES, in case you discover some items you've overlooked!

1. STORE WATER — HOWEVER YOU CAN.

You probably don't have a lot of room to spare in your home. You may have a separate storage shed somewhere nearby. But however you store it, you need sufficient water and food to carry you through for at least three days, and up to 10 days or 2 weeks is better.

One gallon of water per person per day is the standard. Obviously, water in 5 gallon bottles could fill up most of a closet! And you have to be cautious in how you store large volumes of liquids as a leak could cause serious damage to floors, particularly in older homes where floors are made of mere particle board.

Why not convert all or part of a closet or outdoor shed to an emergency pantry at the very outset? That way, you can set it up properly, with a waterproof floor, shelves, etc.

Some ways to store water:

- Best and most efficient is to store water in a **55 gallon barrel**.* It needs to be positioned up off a concrete floor, and you need to "condition" the water every year. But having that much clean water available will probably solve your emergency water problem entirely.
- Consider **square water "bricks"*** that don't waste any space and lock together. (Each brink is about the size of a large shoebox.) You could

stack them two high, for example, to fit under a bed or on the bottom shelf of a bookcase, or six high in the closet. Better yet, of course, put them in your pantry.

- **Freeze water** in square plastic containers and store them in the freezer. They help keep the freezer efficient and can be an easy source of water when you need it. (The ice can last 2 or 3 days after power is lost.)
- If you have advance warning of a storm or other emergency, store additional water in your **bathtub**.* There's a bathtub liner designed just for that.
- Consider **collapsible water bottles*** that you can fill at the last minute -- very inexpensive, easy to store, very practical.

*You can see examples of all these and a lot more at our website. Go to https://emergencyplanguide.org and just type the word "water" into the search bar at the upper right of each page.

You and your pets MUST have water to survive!

In case you have to carry water from another location to your home, be sure to have some sort of container that you can manage with one hand. (The other hand holds the flashlight – or the railing.) A 2-3 gallon container is probably about right. Anything smaller wastes your energy; anything larger may be too heavy to manage, particularly if you are going up stairs.

Real Life: Does your community have a swimming pool? It may be a real resource – as water for flushing toilets, even some cleaning, but not for drinking. We even looked into using our pool water to fight fires and discovered it would require a huge pump with generator and yards of hose, plus trained people to manage the whole apparatus. Not realistic.

2. FOOD IS A NECESSITY.

You probably always have some food supplies on hand, but follow the advice of survival experts: Store what you eat, eat what you store. (Build up a supply of favorite foods in the cupboard; eat from the front, replenish at the back — on a regular basis.)

Supplement your usual canned items with freeze-dried or packaged dried-food supplies; they are small and light.

However, note that most freeze-dried or "instant" foods require water and cooking.

If you're thinking of using your charcoal-burning BBQ to heat water for cooking these freeze-dried meals – only use it outside! A propane camping stove may be OK for short periods inside as long as you have plenty of ventilation. In either case, you'll need to store some fuel for the stove.

Cooking on any emergency stove inside your home puts you at risk for carbon monoxide poisoning! Carbon monoxide is odorless and colorless and puts you to sleep, never to wake up. Don't let it happen to you or your family.

Real Life: A June, 2017 news headline reads: "FIVE people hit a snag after cooking on a barbecue indoors, suffering suspected carbon monoxide poisoning. The three women and two men, aged from their teens into their 50s, developed headaches and nausea after using the barbecue inside for about four hours."

You won't have to worry about this if your emergency food requires no cooking at all.

With your food supplies, don't forget a manual can opener and a knife for opening plastic or foil containers, and a spoon to eat with. Pack and store these in that pantry.

In a real emergency, local stores' inventory will disappear amazingly fast, and even trying to shop for food may be dangerous. Remember that it takes electricity to power ATMs, cashier terminals and, yes, gasoline pumps. It's best to have enough dry or canned food at home so you don't have to go out unless or until it's safe. (Keep your car's gas tank ½ to ¾ full all the time.)

3. "THE DOCTOR IS OUT."

You may not be able to get to a pharmacy and even if you can, their electricity may be out, just like gas stations, super markets and ATMS. They won't be able to check records or accept payment, so try to keep at least a week's worth of prescriptions on hand at all times.

We have found that many doctors will renew a prescription only a few days before you run out of your supply. We need to help them get past that limitation! Check out our website for more suggestions about getting emergency supplies of medicines, often considered "the missing link" in emergency planning.

Perhaps it's almost needless to say, but I'll say it anyway. Get a good **first aid kit** and add other items you know your family might need, including sunscreen, antibiotic ointment, etc. Also important – update your kit every so often! We've all experienced band aids that no longer stick, small bottles with liquid contents totally dried up, etc.

4. "CAN YOU HEAR ME NOW?" EMERGENCY COMMUNICATIONS.

When the electricity goes out, so does T.V., phone service, and cable internet. So does the door buzzer and the entrance gate call system. You may have some sort of smartphone connection but only so long as your batteries last.

In a big storm, cell phone towers are downed, so your cell phone doesn't work, either, even if you DO have battery power.

Thus emergency preparations need to include a battery-operated radio so you can get official news. The best radios have batteries that can be recharged via hand-cranking or solar. (We study popular emergency radios being sold on Amazon. Check out the latest list here https://emergencyplanguide.org/reviews/emergency-radio-reviews/ Hint: the first one on the list is our favorite!)

Many of the new emergency radios also connect to computers, tablets and smart phones, so if your radio has a solar panel you might be able to charge one of your devices.

5. EMERGENCY LIGHTING.

Most of us have experienced electricity outages, so we know how dramatic they can be even when announced in advance. With no light coming in the window from streetlights, and no lights inside your damaged home, you have no choice but to curl up and stay still until daylight comes.

With limited light, though, you can move confidently, prepare your surroundings to be as comfortable as possible, and feel more normal. All it takes is some planning.

A **flashlight stored in every room** is the rule in our house. We also have **battery-operated lanterns*** that, when set in the middle of the room, light it up completely, if not brightly. Naturally, a supply of batteries for all these lights is essential.

So your emergency pantry needs to include extra batteries — and of the right size. You might also look for solar-powered lights and/or battery chargers.

Until you know it's safe, candles are not advised! Striking a match can set off a gas explosion! And candles easily burn down and/or tip over. Be extra cautious with their use . . . especially if there is any chance of a natural gas leak in your home or neighborhood.

Check the Appendix for more on lighting and lanterns.

6. WITHSTANDING THE WEATHER.

You home's heating system, whether electrical or gas, is likely to go down and stay down in an emergency.

You probably don't have the luxury of burning wood in a fireplace, and a home generator* can be cumbersome, require storage of fuel, and frequent starting for maintenance. (In a spacious park, you might find a generator desirable for emergency power. But remember, you can't plug it into the electrical system for your house!)

If you live in a cold climate, invest in a cold-weather sleeping bag. There's nothing as effective.

Have a good pair of boots, a cold-weather coat you can put over other layers, and a rain poncho. Even in sunny southern California, where we live, it can get very cold very quickly at night, and many people don't have adequate clothing if they're not protected by a snug house.

We talked about stoves before. You may be able to use a propane camping stove for cooking, as long as you have adequate ventilation. A cup of hot soup, hot chocolate or coffee will be mighty welcome.

But do not leave an open flame burning for room heating.

As mentioned before, any emergency stove you do have will require fuel that will also have to be stored.

Before you plan for any improvised heating or cooking we strongly urge you to get advice from your local fire authority.

7. REPAIRING DAMAGE.

Depending on the situation, you may have to make repairs to your home to keep it habitable. Some essential tools:

- Flashlight and lantern
- Hammer, nails
- Gloves, safety glasses or goggles, headlamp
- Duct tape, visqueen sheet plastic
- Utility knife with variable blades and tools
- Pliers (a multi-tool?), heavy-duty scissors or cutters
- Pry bar
- Screw drivers (Phillips head and slot head)

Obviously, there's no use collecting tools you don't know how to use. But maybe a neighbor DOES know how to put them to use! More on that in Part Two.

And you'll have to use your judgment about cutting, hammering or taping doors, walls and windows. Damages to property you don't own must be weighed against the steps you feel you must take to protect your family.

8. SANITATION.

This is likely to be one of your biggest challenges, but critical for health. If the entire neighborhood has been hit by the emergency, you can assume that it will only take a couple of hours before your toilet will no longer flush and will begin to back up.

The only solution: **heavy-duty trash compactor plastic bags*** placed either in the toilet or in a five-gallon bucket, that once filled with waste is carried outside to be disposed of at some designated spot. Regular plastic bags won't do, but if that's all you have, double them up.

Dealing with human waste is yukky and can even be dangerous. A supply of toilet paper and paper towels needs to be augmented with rubber gloves and sanitary wipes to be sure you are able to clean up any spills. It's a good idea to have a jug of Clorox or other disinfectant available so you can pour some on discarded waste.

"WHAT ABOUT THE NEIGHBORS?"

Living in a mobilehome park, you'll have to consider your neighbors in an emergency. To a certain extent, you will all be in the same boat and dependent on one another for basic survival.

- Do you even know your closest neighbors? Will they be able to help themselves?
- Will they be able to help you?
- Will they turn to you for help?
- Or will they turn ON you for help?

If you're not sure about the answers to these questions, you'll get more ideas in Part Two. Just keep reading!

NOTES ON PERSONAL PLANNING

What items are you missing? Do you have a family? Survival gear makes great and thoughtful presents! Jot down your ideas here!

Part Two: Counting on your Neighbors

When the tsunami hit in Japan in 2011, people were pulled alive out of wrecked homes not because they were able to signal their location to First Responders, but because neighbors knew where they should have been and went looking for them!

We saw neighbors in action in Mexico City after the September 2017 earthquake, too.

It was the personal connections and concern for one another that made the difference for these people, not the size of the home or how rich the resident was.

Living in a mobilehome community, you and your neighbors will likely face the same challenges . . .

- Some people will be away or commuting and struggling to get home.

- Some people will be at home, trying to connect with distant family members.
- Some homes may be damaged more than others.
- The entire park may be threatened with gas leaks, flooding, or power outages.
- We believe that fire is the most serious threat to residents in mobilehome parks. This is because of the age of the parks (i.e., old-fashioned piping, buried shallowly) and because older mobile homes are constructed with highly flammable materials. Our First Responders figure an older home will burn i[completely within 10 minutes. Unfortunately, we have seen it happen in our own park more than once.
- Emergency supplies that you or your neighbors have dutifully stashed away may be destroyed or unavailable.

Whatever the situation, if you are prepared and willing to help each other, you may be able to prevent the emergency from turning into a widespread disaster.

So how do you go about being "prepared and willing to help each other?"

We see this as a three-step process.

STEP 1. PREPARE YOURSELF FIRST.

Your first responsibility is to yourself and your family. Part One of this report, that you have already read, lists some of the supplies that you will need to survive in an extended disaster.

You will want to add other things to the list, too, such as baby items, sanitary items, personal items like prescription glasses, etc. Many complete checklists are available online, from the Red Cross, the Federal Emergency Management Agency (FEMA) or your own city. The very first item of the Appendix of this book is an extended list that we have put together with our neighbors.

Real Life: As it turns out, you won't be happy with just one list for assembling supplies. We've had to come up with several lists. For example, our first list is the 3-Day Survival Kit List. The second list we call the Shelter-In-Place List, which considers your needs for getting along on your own for 10 days to 2 weeks. And then there's the Evacuation List. To make it even tougher, all your kits will be different from everybody else's, because you're unique! Just build them the best you can!

An important item in every list of supplies is your **Emergency Contact List and Family Communications Plan**.

Build a chart that shows where your family members are likely to be. Come up with ways for all of you to contact each other in an emergency. Include an out-of-town friend or relative on your list of contacts, because outbound texts or calls may get through when local calls don't.

Naturally, if you have young children your contact list will be different from an adult's. There's plenty more about Family Communications Plans online and at our website.

So, Step One in any survival planning may mean simply making sure that everyone in the mobilehome park gets a simple, useful emergency supplies checklist. The park owner, manager or

Homeowners' Association should be willing to help duplicate and distribute the list.

One addition reality. Unless you are actively taking steps to prepare your own family, you'll have little credibility when you try to get others to take action!

Real Life: Occasionally we help our local fire department do outreach for emergency preparedness. It has included handing out emergency supplies lists at local grocery stores. In a couple of locations, we provide reminders in more than one language. What languages are spoken in your community? Adjust as possible. This is not the time to be an English language purist.

STEP 2. GET COMMUNITY EMERGENCY RESPONSE TEAM (CERT) TRAINING FOR YOURSELF AND A CORE TEAM.

One important thing that FEMA has done since it was created in 1979 is set up free training for citizens so they can assist others in an emergency. CERT training typically takes place in a classroom and in the field, with classes taught by professional members of the local fire department and police.

The entire course takes 24 hours. Graduates come out with knowledge, having practiced some moves and some decision-making, plus they receive some basic emergency equipment: helmet, gloves, safety glasses, etc.

There is no cost for this training!

There is a lot more about CERT in the Appendix. First, though, find out whether your city offers CERT training. If it doesn't, you can get the training online at FEMA.gov. (See the link in the Appendix.)

There is no substitute for CERT training.

We could never have built our neighborhood team without CERT.

Everyone in the course learns the same basic information and comes out able to work together and "speak the same language" of emergency response. When you've all taken the course, everyone is equally important and can take on the same leadership roles.

STEP 3. INTRODUCE THE CONCEPT OF A NEIGHBORHOOD TEAM.

Once you and your core group have the credibility of being CERT graduates, the next step is to begin organizing your neighbors – including your property manager or property owner.

If management has already made plans for how employees are to respond in an emergency, it will be invaluable to have them at your meeting, too. (Generally, whatever planning has been done by management will be only for evacuation procedures. It won't include planning for assisting residents to shelter-in-place.)

We know from experience that people WILL come out for an "informational meeting" if they . . .

- See a value to them personally
- Understand what to expect
- Are invited properly and often.

So start your organizing by setting up a community or neighborhood meeting to "Discuss emergency response in our park."

Your invitation needs to be carefully drafted so it includes the bulleted information above. And feel free to suggest that people who don't show up and who don't prepare in advance will suffer more when the emergency hits . . .!

See the Appendix for a simple, sample invitation.

STEP 4. HOLD ONGOING INFORMATIONAL MEETINGS AND TRAININGS.

After the first meeting, develop a series of informal get-togethers to engage and involve more and more of your neighbors. At every meeting, stress the importance of them getting CERT training.

Real Life: CERT classes may not be held regularly, and they may be overbooked. At every neighborhood meeting, we pass out the schedule of upcoming classes and encourage neighbors to "get on the waiting list." When we can, we celebrate a recent graduate, too - have the graduate say a few words about the course and show off his or her green CERT gear.

The purpose of all the local meetings is to gather interested neighbors together so they can assess their risks, take stock of their strengths, and above all, begin to know each other!

Planning regular meetings takes some thought and a lot of follow-through. You may need to bring in guest experts – perhaps someone from the local police, fire department or CERT organization. Consider inviting someone from the Red Cross or the local Humane Society; they have outreach objectives they have to meet, remember!

And of course experienced meeting planners know the value of refreshments!

Here are **five simple agenda ideas** to get started:

1. Plan a "show and tell" of emergency equipment.
2. Show "how-to" videos from the internet.
3. Tour your park and/or clubhouse, noting fire extinguishers, exits, etc.
4. Hear stories from attendees of "emergencies I've been through."
5. Share and discuss a quiz or checklist.

And here are **four more agenda ideas** that will fall into place naturally as neighbors connect and feel ever more comfortable:

1. Share good ideas (how you've developed a Family Communications Plan, or converted a closet into a storage space).
2. Take stock of special needs and special skills within the group (medical needs, construction skills and tools, etc.).
3. Come up with ideas for buying in bulk, supplementing each other's supplies.
4. Train people on how to use their emergency radios or other equipment.

We have helped put on monthly meetings nearly every month for 15 years – that's over 150 meetings! I even assembled a collection of "Meeting Ideas for Neighborhood Groups." There's a link to the **Meeting Ideas book** in the Appendix.

STEP 5. ACTIVELY RECRUIT GROUP MEMBERS.

People who are attracted to your meetings are the ones who are most likely to become members of your neighborhood team.

But guess what!

They probably won't volunteer UNLESS THEY ARE ASKED!

You may have to talk to people individually, to find out what their interest and skills are, and what they are worried about when it comes to emergencies.

With that information, you can extend an invitation to become a member of the team. Even if they haven't gone through the formal CERT training, neighbors can become important team members as long as they receive a simple orientation.

It will also help your recruiting efforts to have some simple items to present to new members, like an inexpensive flashlight, a tablet and pen, etc. We also give all our active members a vest and a name tag.

Real Life: Many times, when we've asked people to join in our neighborhood group, we have heard this response. "Oh, I don't have time to be a part of the group, but if something happens, you can count on me to help."

This is tough to counter. The only answer I've found is, "But how will you know WHAT TO DO?" Eager but untrained "helpers" may be more of a hindrance than a help. Members of the team face any emergency with a better understanding of what to expect and how best to respond. They don't start off clueless.

STEP 6. DEVELOP THE TEAM.

Ultimately, your goal is to develop a basic Emergency Preparedness Plan for your community.

As you build your team, the Plan will build itself.

There are standard recommendations for building a Plan, but even without a full-fledged one, whatever you can do to raise individual awareness and build readiness to work as a group will make your entire community safer.

Part Three, coming up, will get you started on the Plan.

NOTES ON TEAM BUILDING

Who would be a great guest speaker for your community? Which of your neighbors could reach out and invite that person? Come up with a list of a half-dozen people so you start with a strong line-up.

Part Three: Building Your Neighborhood Plan

I n the event of a major catastrophe –
an earthquake, a hurricane, a widespread grid failure -- local businesses
and neighborhoods simply won't be able
to count on timely help from fire
departments or emergency services.

We need to be self-sufficient because,
for the first hours and even days
following a disaster, rescue personnel
and equipment will be overwhelmed.

Immediately following a disaster, First
Responders will be busy surveying their
entire geographic area of responsibility
and reporting on damages and
immediate needs. They may be occupied
with higher priority missions (hospitals,
civic centers, schools, police stations,
retirement homes, etc.). Or they could be
physically unable to respond due to

blocked or damaged roads, downed bridges, or other obstructions.

You and your neighbors are the true First Responders! The quality of your response to the emergency will be the key to your survival.

The success of your response will depend on the preparations you have already made. There will be no time for training once an emergency arises.

As you might expect, building a team and managing training is not easy. And there's no one right way to proceed. What follows are suggestions from our own experience or research.

Realize you can't build a plan by yourself.

You'll need to identify leaders in your community – other people willing to "buy in" and take ownership.

What follows are some logical actions that concerned residents can take to build a team and a plan. They assume that at least ONE person – you? -- steps up to start the process. They also assume that you will find other neighbors who want to be part of a well-intentioned and well-run group.

Focus on the important things first. A partially-completed plan is better than no plan.

ON YOUR OWN, OR WITH A NEIGHBOR OR TWO . . .

Find out if a plan already exists.

Ask management or past community leaders: "Do we have an Emergency Plan? A Contingency Plan? An Evacuation Plan?"

There's no use trying to reinvent the wheel or contradict plans that have been made by others.

(There may be no plan. But find out before you make any assumptions.)

Identify everybody who has responsibility for any aspect of your park.

This may include property owners, management, local authorities, utility companies, maintenance, security, etc. If it's a resident-owned complex, find out what decisions the Board has made or makes about special insurances, safety features (sprinklers, warning systems), etc.

Put together a master list, with names and contact info. All these people will be considered in your planning.

Start your educational library.

Depending on your community, you may find many materials to be too complex or filled with too much jargon. Still, build a training library. You or others will be able to use these as resources and for credibility. Don't overlook online CERT training.

With the core group, preferably all CERT graduates, continue your investigation.

Identify potential threats.

This can readily be done in just one brain-storming session!

Look at risks posed by the location itself (perched on an eroding cliff; next to a busy highway), threats associated with manufacturing or production in your community (chemicals, fertilizers, paints), transportation threats due to airports, railroads or ports, etc.

Naturally, you'll be aware of threats from natural causes, too: rain, flooding, hurricanes, tornados, etc..

Add everything to the list!

After the brainstorming, take another run through the threats and rank them in order of severity and likelihood of occurrence.

You'll refer back to this information as you begin to attract more members to your group.

Real Life: We've mentioned it already once, but fires from broken gas lines are of particular danger to mobilehome communities. When there's a break, gas may escape anywhere. If residents jump in their cars to flee the park, but are trapped in a traffic jam, the heat from automotive catalytic converters will ignite more fires. During the 1994 Northridge quake a whole park burned to the ground this way. Making residents understand this threat presents a major educational challenge to every mobilehome emergency response team.

Find out about legal obligations.

The park owner and management may be required to prepare emergency plans.

They may not be required to commit to protecting residents. This may vary in every state or city. Begin to think about how to enlist support from the owners and managers to meet their moral and legal obligations. (This may not be as easy as you'd think. Managers may feel you are challenging their competence or encroaching on their turf. Approach carefully!)

Investigate financial assistance.

If you pay association or homeowners' dues, maybe the organization can set aside a few dollars a month from each resident. Non-profit organizations may be able to apply for grants. All this is preliminary – but we know that it takes at least some money to run a group.

Check with local fire and police about evacuation protocols.

Shelter-in-place is the preferred survival tactic for many emergencies, but evacuation may be necessary. Visit your local fire station and ask: What are likely evacuation routes and where are likely shelters? While you're there, find out how far they are away from your community, and how long it generally takes for them to respond.

Ask to find out if they have had previous experience with your location that is important for you to know about.

Real Life: Wildfires are a danger here in California, particularly after years of draught. It turns out that "fire corridors" -- similar to "tornado alleys" -- burn over and over again. Your fire department will be able to tell you about your location.

Confer with your utility providers.

It's good to know where gas and power lines are located, where shut-offs are, whether your complex has automatic shut-offs, etc. (Your community may be served by the local utility and/or a private utility company.) Generally residents won't have occasion to take steps to shut off utilities, but they might if managers or utility workers aren't available. (Once again, be aware that information about utilities may be difficult to obtain. Utility services are sensitive to sabotage and tend to be vague about details.)

It's when you begin assembling the data, asking the questions and researching your neighborhood that the shadowy impressions of what it would be like in an emergency start coming into sharper focus!

At first, you're really collecting a lot of raw data at random. A box with file folders to organize things in is a good, transferable idea. (Not everyone will use the same computer programs.)

OK, that's the homework for stage one. You may have done most of this yourself! But now, it's . . .

TIME TO GET MORE NEIGHBORS INVOLVED.

Here is a suggested approach that will help keep things organized. Lay it out for all your group members so they can volunteer support where it makes sense.

Legal Caution: Your neighborhood CERT group starts and remains a volunteer organization. It does not take on any responsibility for protecting the residents of the community; its goal is to educate and encourage residents to prepare themselves and understand the value of helping their neighbors. As a

CERT "Leader" you have no authority other than the goodwill you can develop.

What you will see over the next few pages seems simple. It IS simple – but it will take time. The good news: every single step forward adds to your chances of getting safely through an emergency.

Define your territory.

Start with a map of the property and neighborhood that shows buildings, common areas, parking as well as entry and exit points. Could exits and entrances be improvised if the main entrance is blocked? (Don't worry about all the details at this point. You're only in the beginning stages.)

Include the location of fire extinguishers, fire hydrants and utility shut-offs.

You will probably have to draw the map yourself.

See if you can find out what emergency symbols are used in your area so you use the same ones to show the location of elevators, fire alarms, fire extinguishers, stairwells, etc.

Once your map is drawn, you can take a photo or scan it so it can be shared digitally.

Review your list of threats.

You've already done some work on threats, but now's the time to get all your neighbors involved. This is a great topic for a group meeting.

Risks vary by location. Probably everybody knows about threats from the weather; either you live in a flood plain or you don't. If you're in an area safe from earthquakes but on the edge of a forest with high fire danger, you have different priorities than a property bordered by mainline train tracks or in the flight path of a local airport.

Do you have tunnels or bridges on the property? Elevators? Do you have children or pets, aged or physically impaired residents? People who only speak languages other than English? All these can be considered "threats," risks or impediments that need to be considered.

(We have added a comprehensive list of risks to the Appendix. You can use it to help prompt more discussion, if needed!)

Once you've listed all the threats you can think of, go to the second step of prioritizing them. That is, what is the likelihood of something happening, and what is the likely result?

Again, this is only the beginning, so rough estimates are all that you need.

Real Life quick question: What happens to your perimeter gates or parking gates in a power outage?

I'll bet your group members already know the answer to this one!

Identify your assets.

How close are you to fire and police stations? What kinds of businesses (if any) are close by? What is the status of the water supply in the park? How many residents are able-bodied? How many retired? How many arc likcly to be available in an emergency?

How many people with first aid or medical experience? How about people skilled in trades? What tools are available? How about working vehicles (trucks, vans, etc.)? Motorhomes (with AC electrical supply generators)? Boats? Snow blowers? Golf carts?

What kind of mutual interests do you share with nearby businesses, churches, restaurants, etc.?

In your first meetings, you can only estimate the answers to some of these questions. At the beginning, people may be reluctant to share details of personal information.

At a later date, when your neighbors have heard about the Emergency Response Team are more comfortable with the idea of working together, you may be able to use a survey to capture more complete answers.

Naturally, you will also have to have a **plan for protecting the privacy** of this information. (In some places, management may already have a list of residents with disabilities. They may not be able to share this list, so your resident group will have to come up with its own. As long as neighbors understand and trust the group, they are likely to be willing to offer this kind of information.)

Divide into zones and teams.

Now we want to figure out how to share the responsibilities.

Based on the number of residents and the campus layout, divide the map into zones or divisions.

Teams will be set up to help residents in each division. How many teams will you need?

For example, a division might consist of 30-60 homes, headed up by a Division Leader. Then, for each 10 or so units, you want one person who knows the people and can check on them in an emergency. This is the Block Captain. (A "Block" is a group or block of homes. There's more on the role of the Division Leader and the Block Captains coming up.)

Build your preliminary organization chart.

Somebody has to take charge of each activity. Your organization chart lays it out.

We have found that the best way to build your chart is to draw it with empty boxes first and fill in names as you get volunteers.

None of this will happen overnight. It will take time to identify people with the interest and the skills you want.

But don't ever be concerned about over-staffing! (Just squeeze another name into that box!) You simply can't have too many people on your teams. As we've said before, major emergencies and disasters aren't predictable. Probably 10-25% of your team/s will be away from home when an event occurs.

Having extra people as backup or "Reserves" can make all the difference.

Diagram 1 at the end of this chapter shows sample Leadership Teams. The titles and positions follow CERT guidelines.

Your list of special teams will depend on the size and make-up of your complex. Smaller parks may be able to consolidate their teams. Larger complexes, on the other hand, may find it necessary to have more than one special team.

Here are common special teams:
- Communications
- Fire, Search and Rescue
- Triage and First Aid
- Damage Report and Control (Building Safety)
- Care and Shelter (Including Child Center and Pet Care units)
- Property Security

- Logistics /or Auxiliary Power
- Transportation

You won't always be able to staff up for every division or special team. Do the best you can! (And don't forget people may want to move from one team to another.)

NOW, TIME TO STAFF UP!

The core of the Plan – Block Captains.

We've started with a look at leadership (you and your core group), and while leadership is essential, your plan will really depend on the people "on the ground," those who have agreed to watch out for their immediate neighbors and be the conduit for information, education, etc.

These are the Block Captains in each Division. These are the people you're seeking to recruit and engage at monthly meetings!

Diagram 2 at the end of this chapter shows what the Block Captains and Division Team plan looks like.

A Block Captain has a simple but essential job. In an emergency, Block Captains follow a few, simple steps.

First, they check on their own safety and the condition of their family.

Second, they check on the condition of their home to see whether it is safe.

Third, they check on their immediate neighbors. Typically, each Block Captain has 10 or so neighbors to check on. Obviously, the more he or she knows about the neighbors, the easier it will be to anticipate whether the home is empty, who might be in there needing help, etc.

Fourth, the Block Captains report in to their Division Leader on the status of their Block. If they need help, they request it. In most cases, this communication can take place via walkie-talkies. These hand-held devices will work even when all other communications are down!

We have found that finding and keeping Block Captains is the toughest job of all, in part because you need more of them than anything else!

Note: We've included a short Block Captain's Checklist in the Appendix. You'll need back-up Block Captains and every Block Captain must be ready to step up and act as Division Leader if necessary. Let everyone train for more than one role!

Division Leaders

The number of divisions in your community will depend on its size and make-up. Each division will have a Division Leader who transmits information from the Block Captains to Command and Control, and then back again from Command to the Block Captains.

Command and Control

At the center of your team is Command and Control. When an event happens, the Incident Commander sets up a headquarters and directs, with the help of Control (head of communications or Net Control) the other teams to where they are needed most urgently.

Note: CERT training teaches everyone how to lead the team because the first qualified person on the scene takes on the role of leader.

Command is usually held by one person. Control could be handled by the

Commander, but is preferably handled by a second person. A lot of information is processed and the command center and decisions have to be made quickly. And every decision impacts the future decisions you make because people and resources are being tied up that won't be available until tasks are completed.

It actually takes a whole team to make the Command and Control function work smoothly. Choosing your Incident Commander and Assistant Incident Commander is important, but everyone on the Command and Control Team needs to be prepared to fill that role. You just don't know who will be available and first on the scene.

Fire, Search and Rescue Team

This team may have to step in only if professional First Responders aren't available. And this team stands down when First Responders arrive and take over.

In their absence, however, the team's role is a challenging one.

Fighting fires can be especially dangerous and usually involves preventive measures to keep a fire from spreading or to remove people from approaching flames.

Likewise, Search and Rescue must be approached carefully.

All too often, untrained rescuers become part of the problem, despite their good intentions. Even professional firefighters approach rescues cautiously.

There are proven techniques to safely performing "light" search and rescue operations, and usually certain tools are required. These team members must know how to instruct and direct others to help them perform their mission.

Once again, CERT training will give these team members basic information they need. And working with your local fire department will give you a better understanding of how to assist your neighbors in the case of a fire.

Triage and First Aid Team

In "Triage" we learn to first survey a scene and classify the seriousness of injuries, treating only those injuries that are quick and easy to handle. People who are near death or require major medical help are attended to only after we've assessed all the victims and mobilized those that are able to care for themselves and possibly help with others.

This may appear illogical at first, and may even be hard to follow. Our first instinct is to help when someone is seriously injured!

But by treating the most minor injuries first, we are doing the most good for the greatest number of people. And, we spare ourselves the trauma of dealing later with people whose minor injuries have now become major ones.

Triage is really the "assessment" process. It may include getting injured people to a central location where their injuries can be looked after by the team with the most medical training.

Not every community will have trained medical personnel in its ranks. All you can do as volunteers is learn some basic first aid and apply common sense.

Time for our first legal warning: Check out your state's Good Samaritan laws. They offer legal protection to volunteers trying to help in an emergency. CERT training may add additional protection – but it may not. Be sure you know who and what is covered!

Damage Assessment and Control

Determining how seriously a mobilehome is damaged is an important step in deciding if it is safe for residents to remain inside. It's also important to assess whether a home presents danger to neighboring homes or buildings.

A mobilehome may be totally demolished, but more often, individual units are destabilized only enough to trap residents.

Real Life*:* When the 1989 San Francisco earthquake hit, I was meeting in a restaurant making final plans for a class we were giving across the street. After we crawled out from under the restaurant table, we made our way outside and headed for home. Everything LOOKED OK from the outside. Inside though, we found a complete mess. Everything from the kitchen shelves was on the floor – flour, pickles, plates and glassware, sugar, soy sauce, a toaster. And we couldn't get into one of the bedrooms at all because a bookcase had fallen, blocking the door. We didn't know if the apartment was safe to sleep in that night – so we slept out on the street with the rest of our neighbors!

Having professional builders or other trades people on the Damage Control Team is especially helpful. If you can't tell that a home is safe, err on the side of caution.

Care and Shelter Teams

In a severe emergency, caring for injured or displaced residents can be a huge challenge. In "senior residences" we have larger numbers of aged residents with medical needs or mobility challenges. But, we also are more likely to have a greater pool of retired people who have significant business or trade skills and more of them are likely to be home during the day.

In family parks there may be more able-bodied residents to respond to an emergency, but not during the business day. Also, the presence of more children presents a special challenge.

In both settings, pets can present a separate problem.

The Care and Shelter Teams need to be formed to match the circumstances of the individual complex.

Real Life: There is a natural tendency for residents to gravitate to the office or community center area in an emergency. In fact, your park management team may have been trained to bring people to a central area. Unless immediate evacuation is called for, this is usually not a good idea!

Think about it.

Picture a crowd of people milling about, rumors rampant, maybe inclement weather, no place to sit, toilets overrun, no access to food. It would be far better for people to remain in the familiar surroundings of their own homes (assuming they are safe, of course) where they have extra clothing and a supply of food. Yes, some changes may be necessary, but managing them one at a time will be far easier than dealing with a crowd.

However, you may want to consider setting up a place in each Division where volunteer hosts provide Care and Shelter Areas for children, for pets and for aged residents with medicinal or life support needs.

Security Team/s

Most people think of "security" as protecting residents from vandalism or keeping order. But, this is really a minor activity for most parks that isn't needed in the early stages of an emergency. Chances are good that these services will be available from local authorities by time the need arises.

It's more likely that Security Teams will work with Damage Assessment and Control Teams to cordon off dangerous areas, move RVs into position to supply auxiliary power, direct foot and vehicular traffic and even help arrange for evacuation where appropriate.

Logistics and/or Auxiliary Power Team/s

From supplies to finding alternate sources of power (batteries, generators,* etc.), this is the team to fill in the holes.

Real Life – Setting up and staffing this many teams is a lot of work and may not even be required or possible in your community. No matter how hard we try, we don't have people in every position all the time.

We have listed all the teams here, though, because these are the teams suggested by CERT. Just considering them gives you a better grasp on what your community might face in an emergency.

DIAGRAM 1 – SAMPLE LEADERSHIP TEAMS

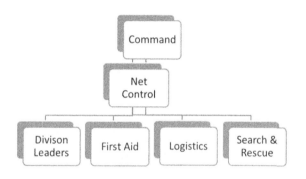

Your chart may look different, depending on the make-up of your community. Add special teams as necessary.

DIAGRAM 2 – SAMPLE EMERGENCY TEAM

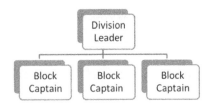

A Division Leader oversees, at most, 50-60 homes. A Block Captain reports on a maximum of 10 neighbors. If your Divisions are large, you may need many Divisions and Block Captains.

NOTES ON STAFFING UP

You'll want a simple **job description** for each position in your organizations chart. Start with the Block Captain. As questions arise during your recruiting process, improve your description. (Before you start recruiting in earnest, be sure to read the section of this book called "What's the Real Payoff.")

NOTES ON STAFFING UP, CONTINUED

Jot down who you think would make a good Block Captain, but remember that people often want to CHOOSE the role they will play, rather than be assigned. Make sure people hear about all the options

In-Depth: Communications, the Critical Component

You've got some teams in place.

How do you direct activities of your teams at a distance, between Divisions and between teams, when phone service is down?

Use the simplest method you can!

- The size and layout of your complex will determine much of your needs. A small park might well get by with a **few bullhorns**.

- A large complex, with several hundred homes, may find the most reliable and cost-effective communications method to be **hand-held radios** (walkie-talkies).

- **HAM radio and CB radios** may be useful in communicating with the outside world, but in a small geographic area may not be practical. HAM radio operators require a license. (Once again, our experience in Puerto Rico has shown the value of ham radio operators. Over 3,800 went into action to support the Red Cross and military operations there.)

WALKIE-TALKIES ARE AN INEXPENSIVE SOLUTION.

Everyone on your team should have a hand-held, battery-operated radio, or walkie-talkie.

These radios are available online and at stores like Target and Costco for anywhere from $15 to $30 each. Because models change, and advertised range may not be accurate, be sure to test a couple of pairs before you buy too many. (If you purchase a variety of models from Amazon "for evaluation," you can trade it unwanted ones.)

We have reviewed walkie-talkies in depth with full descriptions of the differences between them. Check them out:
https://emergencyplanguide.org/reviews/

We have found that the selection is particularly good around the holidays and prices come down after Christmas!

TIERED COMMUNICATIONS ARE REQUIRED.

The division level is where the majority of action will take place in the early stages of an event.

You want your Block Captains to be able to communicate with each other and their Division Leader in their own division. Each division should have its own channel.

Next, you want the Division Leaders to be able to change channels to communicate with the Command center. Command also needs to communicate with the special teams. The Division Leader and Command radios may need to be more powerful to stretch across the entire property, and thus may need to be more expensive.

Assigning channels requires some careful planning after thinking through various scenarios. There's no one right way for all communities.

The Appendix has a chart showing the channel assignments for a two-way radio set-up that we have used successfully in our community. And there's a special offer there too regarding communications.

Under certain circumstances your local walkie-talkie net may be overwhelmed by too much outside traffic. Still, those people probably don't have a plan, and they are likely to quickly run out of batteries. Your plan gives your neighborhood team members a chance to communicate meaningfully.

NOTES ON COMMUNICATIONS

Of course, cell phones are the common emergency communications device. Our group members practice texting and using the various cellphone emergency alerts and apps. But remember, in a BIG emergency, cellphones may not work. Consider alternatives.

In-Depth: The *Written* Contingency Plan

U ltimately, you'll want to draft a written plan that describes your group's set-up and its mission. Only a written plan will.

- Give you credibility with your park owner, insurance company, etc.
- Reassure neighbors, and particularly new neighbors, that you know what you're doing
- Serve as the basis for keeping the emergency program going, year after year, as some neighbors leave and others move in

Of course, not everyone is comfortable being faced with a writing assignment!

But by now, you probably know what your written plan should contain. Keep it simple! All you need are a few tools to pull it all together.

A SAMPLE OUTLINE TO GET YOU STARTED.

Overview – A description of your park, the situation, etc. Why you've put together an Emergency Response Team.

Threat Analysis – Go back to your meeting notes to assemble this information. What is your most likely disaster scenario? Are you in a major fault zone? Near railroad or chemical plants? What about floods? What is most likely to occur that would cause you to mobilize your Emergency Response Team?

Activation Levels – You may want to include specifics here. For example, at what points (Richter scale, local alarms, etc.) do you activate your Command and Control? When do you alert the Division Leaders and Block Captains? Do team members self-activate or wait to be activated? (Remember, they are all volunteers.)

Team Descriptions – How have you decided on Divisions? What are your Special Teams (Fire and Rescue, First Aid and Triage, Damage Control, Security, etc.)? Who is on the teams right now?

(Obviously, lists of team members will have to be updated regularly.)

Procedures – What are the missions of each team and what procedures do they follow in carrying out that mission? At what point do your team members "stand down" and let others (authorities) take over?

Communications Procedures – What is the radio protocol? (Who talks to whom and what is the procedure?) What about radio drills?

Resources – What kind of experience and skills do residents have? What kind of supplies do you have on hand? Where are tools? Etc.

MASTER PLAN VERSUS A SHORTENED MANUAL FOR TEAM MEMBERS.

We have found that our Plan continues to grow and to be updated, year by year, as we learn more about our community, its infrastructure, etc. We keep copies of correspondence, sample training materials, etc. Imagine a binder that just gets thicker and thicker or a file drawer that gets fuller and fuller!

At the same time, we know that new volunteers aren't interested in all this background. For them, we have created a Team Member's Manual that contains just the essentials – a description of the team, map of the neighborhood, basic risks to prepare for, a couple of forms to help Block Captains to capture information about their neighbors, etc.

While nearly all this information is originally created digitally, and stored in a couple of computers, we print out the Team Member Manuals. In an emergency, power may be out and computer materials will therefore be inaccessible.

I think you'll find that as you build your team, your plan will largely build itself.

You don't need one author. In fact, the more people who contribute to building the plan the more likely they will be able to follow it in an emergency. (Let people volunteer to be in charge of one section, for example.)

And again, the reminder that all participants on your team are volunteers and all actions they take will be the result of their own personal decisions.

This is not an official organization. No particular person has the authority to "order" anyone to do anything. Even CERT trained volunteers have no authority to order anyone to take action.

Volunteers respond to people they know and respect. That's why so much effort goes into simply getting neighbors to know one another.

NO EMERGENCY PLAN IS PERFECT OR EVEN COMPLETE.

In fact, you will be lucky if half of your organization and operational strategy work anything like you envision it . . . at least in the early aftermath of an emergency.

Why this pitiful result??

Because, we never really know how or when a disaster will strike! Thus, all the planning and organizing we do is based on assumptions and guesswork.

In a truly major disaster, we don't know who will be home at the time, who may not survive it and which team members, for one reason or another, simply aren't able to do what we expected.

THE PLAN HAS THE BEST CHANCE OF WORKING IF IT'S PRACTICED.

Even with its weaknesses, the plan provides a track for the team to run on and a basis for improvising when the time comes.

When the plan is documented and teams are formed, everything can be tested.

Testing is an ongoing process.

Testing and training can be as simple as a "show and tell" session with people demonstrating what they have in their evacuation bags, or as complicated as an exercise where team members are presented with various "emergencies" in their division and have to decide how to handle them, reporting in by radio as they go.

In the uncertainly of "the real thing," people will instinctively do what they've practiced doing.

This is what we count on! And it's why we put so much effort into the process.

As we have said throughout,

"The better prepared the people are around us, the safer we all will be."

And that is the rationale for Community Emergency Planning in a nutshell!

NOTES ON WRITING THE PLAN

Get a team to help build the table of contents. Get guest writers, with a volunteer editor to keep it all manageable. Keep everything as simple as possible. Store back-up copies in a couple of places.

Results of Your Efforts

We've seen too often what happens when disaster hits.

People are confused, frightened, often shocked into inaction or frenzied indecisiveness. Even when the immediate threat is over, it may take hours before there's a full understanding of what has happened. Some people will be OK, others will need assistance. Some people will step up to help, but on an individual basis.

Disaster may simply overwhelm the community.

A neighborhood emergency response team could change that!

Here's what your team efforts could accomplish:

- Many neighbors will understand quickly what has happened and already have an idea of what they should do next.

- Block Captains will go into action immediately to assess the condition of their neighbors' homes and health, and will send in their report to the group leader.
- Ham radio operator/s will forward that report to authorities.
- After the initial alarm, neighbors will be ready to help out where possible and where necessary – including managing debris, stopping leaks, providing first aid, shepherding children, comforting people who need comforting, etc. If other communications are out, volunteers will be directed via walkie-talkie messages from a central Command.
- If there's a delay in official help arriving, most people will have their own supplies of food, water and emergency lighting. They will expect to shelter in place.
- When First Responders arrive, they will be handed an updated report of who needs immediate help.
- Neighborhood team members will continue to support First Responders and other emergency

aid groups until their services are no longer needed.

We can't stop disasters from happening. But when people are ready both emotionally and physically, the impact of the disaster can be lessened and recovery can start sooner. This is what building a resilient neighborhood is all about.

What's the Real Payoff?
(Tools for Recruiting)

There are a number of reasons why you might want to work with your community to build a Neighborhood Emergency Response Team.

Many reasons are sensible and probably appeal to most people, so you can mention them as you work on recruiting for your team.

Some are probably more like excuses than reasons. These you may wish to be a bit more private about!

Either way, here are some of the payoffs we've experienced, and payoffs that members of our team have admitted to. Which would be of value to you?

GETTING YOUR OWN HOUSE IN ORDER.

You probably already have a good handle on your emergency supplies and preparations – otherwise, you wouldn't have been attracted to this book. But as you work with neighbors, you will naturally put finishing touches on your basic supplies. You can't be talking about the necessity for being able to light a fire without having the tools yourself! Being part of an active group is motivating!

GETTING RELUCTANT FAMILY MEMBERS INVOLVED.

Many families admit to an unbalanced approach to preparedness. That is, one person really supports the idea, but the partner may not. As you talk with neighbors, planning meetings and trainings, everyone in your family will be exposed to the concept of readiness. Knowing that others are supporting the concept makes it easier for reluctant family members to get aboard.

HONESTLY FEELING SAFER.

The more you learn about the property and the people where you live, the more comfortable you'll be about handling mishaps or emergencies. This sense of confidence is a BIG benefit of building a team; you just don't get it when you're limited to just your own family in your own home.

MAKING FRIENDS.

We find that some of our team members participate because they think it's sensible. (These are the same people who change the oil in their cars, get regular dental check-ups, etc. You know them!) Others see members of the group as valued peers, and some find real friendships. (New neighbors will find the chance to make friends particularly valuable. Invite them to join in!) If the emergency hits when you're away from home, you can count on your family members being safer when they are surrounded by knowledgeable and caring friends.

SHARING YOUR EXPERIENCE.

With a life-time behind you, you surely have skills that will be appreciated by this team. Share them! This isn't a place where you have to compete. Just as your neighbors benefit from your experience, you benefit from theirs.

FOLLOWING UP ON A PASSION.

When you have a built-in audience eager to hear more about some aspect of survival planning, it's an invitation for you to become the expert! (Here's where that word "excuse" comes in!) Some proficiencies we've watched develop: HAM radios and radio communications; earthquake science; first aid, etc. And at home, our work with the group justifies acquiring a collection of "tactical tools," some of which we describe and even recommend to our neighbors from time to time.

BEING IN THE KNOW

Some people – and we admit to being in this category – are curious about everything that goes on around them. How things work, who is in charge, what decisions are being made, etc. Members of the Emergency Response Team end up knowing A LOT about their community! In fact, it's the very best way to find it out.

DEVELOPING LEADERSHIP SKILLS.

The preparedness group can use a whole lot of help at a whole lot of levels: organizing meetings, technical assistance (Training people how to change the batteries in their Walkie-talkies!), writing up procedures, managing publicity. Building a team gives everyone a chance to step-up their game to the extent they want.

REACHING THE WIDER COMMUNITY.

Our CERT training has involved us in various city-wide police activities and fire department trainings. We've attended and even testified at various political hearings. And winning the first Annual Community Preparedness Award was great for us – and hopefully it inspired other neighborhoods, too. Not that awards are necessary, but they keep up enthusiasm and motivate new people to join. Nearly every month, our members forward good ideas and worksheets to family members all across the country. ("The more we all know, the safer we all will be!")

GIVING BACK.

Everything you learn through your group activities will apply for the rest of your life – and for the rest of other group members' lives, too. In fact, if your team becomes a part of the fabric of the community, the community will benefit for years to come even after you're gone. There aren't many opportunities where "giving back" can have such an impact. Many of our members cite this as their main motivation for participating.

As you read the next few sections . . .

Keep this quote from Howard Ruff in mind:

IT WASN'T RAINING
WHEN NOAH BUILT THE ARK.

Appendix

BASIC LIST OF EMERGENCY SUPPLIES FOR INDIVIDUALS

As you will see, this list has been divided into three parts: essentials for the first 72 hours, then additional supplies for a longer-term shelter-in-place scenario, and finally the things you might need if you have to evacuate.

While each list has important supplies, you don't have to assemble everything at one time! Decide to add a few items every week, or every month. And as for gear, consider trying out less expensive gear first, before going for the most expensive version. (You may not be able to use it if it's too complicated or too heavy!)

This list offers a good start to assembling essential emergency supplies. It is only a start, however. As you read through, you'll think of items YOU want to include that will make a difference to you, your family members, and your pets.

Print out the list and go over it with your children or other family members. It's a great way to get them involved in planning and being prepared to act in an emergency.

All three lists need to be thought through and completed BEFORE the emergency hits. There will be no time to do any of this work afterwards.

You can find more information on nearly all these items, including some recommendations for what to buy and where to buy it, at our website.

We also recommend you contact your local city or county disaster planning centers for important details about your own community, its risks and resources.

Basic Emergency Supplies (3-day emergency)

- ☐ First aid kit
- ☐ Fire extinguisher/s
- ☐ Emergency radio
- ☐ Flashlights or lanterns – with extra batteries

- [ ] Water – one gallon of water per day per person
- [ ] Food – extra supplies of your favorite canned foods, with can opener, or instant (no cook) meals and snacks
- [ ] Whistle – signal for help or keep in touch
- [ ] Cash – small denominations
- [ ] Local maps – GPS or Google may be down
- [ ] Tools – multi-tool, crowbar, gas shut-off wrench, hammer
- [ ] Camping supplies – matches in waterproof container
- [ ] Utensils – disposable or non-breakable plates, cups, tableware
- [ ] Clothing – work gloves, rain gear, towels
- [ ] Bedding – extra blankets, space blankets
- [ ] Sanitation supplies – toilet paper, heavy duty trash bags for human waste, disinfectant
- [ ] Personal care items – sanitary napkins, medicines, extra glasses (contact lens solution), toothbrush and tooth paste,

100 · VIRGINIA S. NICOLS

       soap/wet wipes, hearing aid
batteries
- Paper, pens – for communicating with others
- List of important phone numbers including out-of-state contact
- More _____

Shelter-in-Place (10-day to 2-week emergency)

- Everything from above
- Four times more water, long-term food, sanitation supplies
- Medicine – 14 day supply (Sometimes very hard to get. Work with your doctor.)
- Cooking items – camp stove and fuel, pots, bowls, utensils; fire starter, matches in waterproof container
- Emergency shelter – tarp, tent
- Plastic sheets and tape -- to seal spaces for comfort or protection
- Tools – knife, hammer, nails, saw (power tools if source of power)
- Emergency communications – handheld radios (walkie-talkies)

☐ Recharge capacity for radios, phones, lights (solar, hand-crank or generator)
☐ Books, games for children
☐ Generator – needs fuel, too
☐ More _____

Evacuation Kit List

☐ Bag/backpack for storing your evacuation kit – a size/weight you can easily carry, fit on your lap in a bus, etc.
☐ Separate pet container with leash, pet food, contact numbers
☐ Keys – extras for cars, house, office
☐ Flashlight – extra batteries
☐ Emergency radio
☐ Food and water supplies for duration of trip
☐ Extra clothing, blankets
☐ Personal care items from lists above – medicines, in particular
☐ A few books, games, favorite toy
☐ Other valuables – photos
☐ Important papers – contact names and numbers (family, legal, business); copies of ID, social security number, credit

cards, passport, insurance, home and car ownership papers, birth, marriage, death and divorce certificates, wills, deeds, loans; medical records

☐ (NOTE: Originals of many or most of these documents can be stored in a safe deposit box at your bank. You are unlikely to be able to carry all these originals with you in the case of an evacuation! You can also scan important papers onto a flash drive – convenient and easy to manage.)

☐ Cash and credit cards

☐ More _____

LIST OF RISKS

Use this list to prompt discussion for your team. Ultimately you will want to prioritize threats as to LIKLIHOOD and SEVERITY for your own community. Most professionals suggest start by getting prepared for the most likely threats.

Active shooter
Arson
Bomb threat
Bomb blast
Brown out
Cable cut
Chemical spill
Communications failure
Construction
Crime investigation
Drought
Earthquake
Electrical outage
Emergency alert
Employee strike
Epidemic
Evacuation
Explosion
Extreme heat

Fire
Flood
Frozen pipes
Gas line leak
Hail storm
Hazardous materials
Home fire
Household chemical emergency
Hurricane
Ice storm
Insect infestation
Lightning
Landlord conflict
Landslide
Land subsidence
Nuclear explosion
Nuclear power plant leak
Place crash
Pandemic
Power failure
Power surge
Public disturbance
Raw sewage
Rodent infestation
Sabotage
Smoke damage
Snow storm
Terrorism
Theft

Thunderstorm and lightning
Tornado
Train derailment
Tsunami
Vandalism
Vehicle crash
Virus
Volcano
Water supply problem
Wildfire
Wind storm

The threat of a pandemic

Every good list of threats includes "epidemic" or "pandemic," but before 2020 many people had never had any real experience with widespread disease. Now we know a lot more! By its very definition, a pandemic spreads across continents and affects many people. Often, it takes months or years before appropriate medical treatment is developed. In the meanwhile, the best way for citizens to prepare is to . . .

- Stay aware of worldwide health news. Pandemics can start anywhere.
- Practice every day smart routines regarding hygiene, eating and

exercise, avoiding sick people, covering a cough, etc.

- Until we know definitively what behavior to avoid or what actions to take, follow the most conservative recommendations.
- Be prepared to nurse sick people at home. Have extra food and medical supplies.
- Know the symptoms that mean you should take a sick family member to the hospital.

A commonly overlooked threat: Loss of Income

Regardless of the actual cause of a catastrophic event, one result is likely to be interruption of your income or total job loss.

Even if your employer has a Business Continuity Plan in place, the chances of the business surviving are only 40%. No plan? It's almost a given that the business will fail.

This reality doesn't bode well for business owners, employees, suppliers or even customers.

Even when an employer does have an emergency survival plan for the business, that plan may be missing a key component: **being prepared to handle the employees' concern for the safety and well-being of their loved ones.**

This concern is so strong that often even the most senior staff members -- with major responsibility for mission critical functions – have been known to abandon the business altogether, struggling to get home to save family from imagined chaos or danger.

Is there a solution?

In our opinion, the ideal solution is **the coordination or even "integration" of communities.** This can be achieved when . . .

- Company management, staff and employees have all been Community Emergency Response Team (CERT) trained.
- The company has built its emergency preparedness plan around the CERT model.
- All employees' family members have been encouraged or even supported in getting the same CERT training.

The ideal extension of this concept would be for each of the employee's residential neighborhoods to also become CERT-trained communities -- which of course is an unlikely possibility. Nevertheless the mere fact of knowing their families are prepared for major emergencies would enable employees to remain at their work stations longer, helping the company take immediate steps to protect important data and equipment.

And, disciplined communications via telecommunications and/or radio between the company and home would provide employees positive feedback on the condition and circumstances of their family members – again, allowing them to take the actions necessary to preserve the business – and their income.

It's a win/win if it can be accomplished. And it all starts with the emergency survival component of a CERT-based Business Continuity Plan. See **Emergency Preparedness for Small Business,** 4th in our *Neighborhood Disaster Survival Series*

SAMPLE INVITATION TO A COMMUNITY MEETING

"What will happen to us in an emergency???"

Get answers from the experts -- your neighbors!

> Everyone is invited!
> Informational Meeting
> [Date, Time, Place]

In a real emergency we will be counting on each other to make it through.

Join new neighbors, long-time residents and emergency team members for . . .

- Guest Speaker from Fire Department
- Demonstration of home safety upgrades
- "Show and Tell" by recent CERT grads
- Q & A period
- Door prizes!

Call to reserve your place today (so we can plan for refreshments!)   [Name, phone number]

SAMPLE RADIO COMMUNICATIONS PLAN

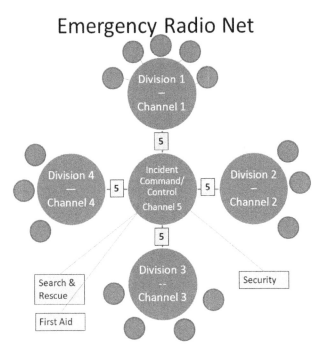

In this simplified plan, each Division has its own radio Channel. Block Captains (small circles) talk to their Division Leader on their own Channel. Command has been assigned Channel 5. Command talks to Division Leaders and to Special Teams on Channel 5.

Special offer for those ready NOW to set up their communications network

If the Radio Net diagram intrigues you, and you don't want to wait to get started setting up a network, use this link to request your free Communications Workbook.

The workbook builds on what you've already read. It includes a discussion of different park/complex layouts, with suggestions for ways to set up your Command Post and Divisions and a method for picking the right radios and assigning channels. It also describes some simple training exercises for your group.

We have found that communications skills are the glue that holds our group together.

BLOCK CAPTAIN'S CHECKLIST

Hand out a simple list like this one to Block Captains so they will know what to do in an emergency. Review the Steps on a regular basis.

BLOCK CAPTAIN'S CHECK-LIST

1. Need fire or police? CALL 911.

2. Check your own home and your immediate neighbors. Safe to continue?

3. Report in to Division Leader by radio on your Division Channel.

4. If no Division Leader, check in with Net Control on Command Channel.

5. Find a partner and check on your 10 block neighbors. Write down their status.

6. Report status to Division Leader or Net Control.

Use your own good judgment and stay safe.

ABOUT CERT

CERT = Community Emergency Response Team

Our neighbors to the north, the City of Los Angeles Fire Department, started the CERT program in 1985. They knew that in the early stages of a catastrophic disaster, citizens would be on their own. Accordingly, LAFD decided that basic disaster survival and rescue skills would help citizens to survive and to help others until other assistance could arrive.

Fast forward to 1994, when FEMA expanded CERT materials to include all hazards and not just earthquakes, and made the program available to communities nationwide. And after September 11, 2001, Citizen Corps was launched and CERT was folded in on the premise that community-based preparedness makes communities more resilient when incidents occur.

- Individuals can prepare homes and families.
- Neighborhoods and worksites can also work together to reduce emergency needs and manage existing resources.

According to the CERT website, around 3,000 groups are actively training CERT members across the country today.

CERT Training

CERT-trained members provide an effective first-response capability. Acting as individuals first, then later as members of teams, trained CERT volunteers can fan out within their assigned areas, extinguishing small fires, turning off natural gas at damaged homes, performing light search and rescue, and rendering basic medical treatment. CERT volunteers also offer a potential workforce to service organizations in non-hazardous functions such as shelter support, crowd control and evacuation.

Course Agenda

The CERT course has a basic agenda, designed to be covered in about 24 hours of classroom and exercise time. Some adjustments may be required to allow for discussion of particular hazards or to allow all participants to take part in class exercise. Topics include:

Disaster preparedness overview
Fire Safety and Utility Controls
Disaster Medical Operations

Light Search and Rescue Operations
CERT Organization and Mobilization
Disaster Psychology
Terrorism and CERT
Final Exam and Disaster Simulation
After the Course

CERT graduates receive basic equipment – vest, goggles, gloves, basic first aid supplies, etc. – and they are encouraged to keep it always available. Team members are also encouraged to participate in continuing supplemental training when it is offered.

All the training and equipment is free to participants.

Real Life: Signing up for CERT may be a bit scary. After all, it's a big commitment, and if most of this subject matter is foreign to you, you may be intimidated. I was – and as the class time got closer and closer, the more insecure I felt!

However, the classes started smoothly, and on time, and just got better and better! Here are some highlights from our training:

Our instructors were active duty and retired police and firefighters, with real experience and good stories to tell. (They have been formally trained to do this teaching.)

Members of the class were a mixed bag – from age 17 up to over 70, men and women, in shape and out of shape, etc. Skill levels were just as mixed.

Much of the training was via lecture (Books were provided.) interspersed with hands-on activities: bandaging a "wound," , putting out a fire, using pry bars to lift "debris" off a body, learning to light and place flares, etc. I had forgotten how much fun it can be to be a member of a team!

Along the way there were quizzes, and the final exam was substantial. Everybody passed, though. And the Disaster Simulation was unexpectedly exciting – trying to find wounded people in a dark and disordered office (furniture tipped over, etc.)!

Since completing the basic training, we have been invited to participate in annual update trainings. Over the years, new subjects have been added to the curriculum – for example, "Run, Hide, Fight" and Terrorism weren't on the list in 2002 when we took the course.

When we return for an update, it's very agreeable to see some familiar faces – people who took the training over 10 years ago, as we did, and who continue to support the program and maintain their own skills. We also have the chance to find out about new survival techniques (new emergency apps), test our own gear (headlamps taped to helmet), etc.

I usually find a way to turn the official update class into a training opportunity for my neighbors who aren't CERT grads or who couldn't make the update.

RESOURCE LIST

At Emergency Plan Guide we turn to a variety of sources for ideas, statistics and stories. Here are a few we recommend.

ESTABLISHED RESOURCES

Community Emergency Response Team training (CERT) (https://www.fema.gov/community-emergency-response-teams)

American Red Cross courses (www.redcross.org/) and

SBA for the small business owner (https://www.sba.gov/managing-business/running-business/emergency-preparedness).

For weather threats and preparedness, the National Oceanic and Atmospheric Administration (http://www.noaa.gov/).

And your State's or city's Office of Emergency Management.

GOOGLE ALERTS

I've set up automated Alerts on several emergency preparedness topics and I get current news stories in my email box every day. Easy to set up and manage – just head to www.google.com/alerts and follow the prompts.

WEBSITES AND SOCIAL MEDIA GROUPS

At Emergency Plan Guide we're interested in neighborhood needs, inspiration for recruiting and facilitating group activities, etc. Your own interests may be very different. In any case, there are many great resources online – websites, blogs, Pinterest pins, Instagram graphics, etc. -- aimed at, for example, survival foods to grow, how to survive in the wilderness, self-defense tactics and weapons, etc. LinkedIn also hosts groups of emergency management professionals that may provide you with a valuable perspective. If you ask a question there you're likely to get some great answers!

EMERGENCY PLAN GUIDE ADVISORIES

We've written well over 300 Advisories mostly devoted to family survival, workplace preparedness or building a neighborhood or workplace team. You'll find all Advisories at our website: https://emergencyplanguide.org/. If you face the challenge of keeping your interest and skills alive, subscribe to our Advisories and you'll get free weekly ideas and training tips, on topics as varied as Best Emergency Radios, Recent Terrorist Activity, The Fire Next Door, What The Heck Is Triage?, Drones Used In Disasters, or How To Escape A Sinking Car. (These have been some of the favorites!)

(Looking for something in particular? Use the search box on every page of the site to get right to it.)

Encourage neighbors to subscribe, too. The Advisories are free, and different people will like different topics and bring their knowledge and enthusiasm to your team-building efforts!

SELECTED SURVIVAL ITEMS

Where you see an asterisk in the text, we have bought and used these items and written in detail about our experiences.

Water –Here are several Advisories on water storage.

Water barrel (comes with hand pump)
https://emergencyplanguide.org/summer-water-shortage/
Contaminated water –
https://emergencyplanguide.org/Dont-drink-that-water/
Swimming pool -
https://emergencyplanguide.org/Emergency-Water-Supply-Your-Swimming-Pool!
Collapsible water bottles -
https://emergencyplanguide.org/collapsible-water-bottles-indispensable-to-survive-a-disaster/
Plastic bottles -
https://emergencyplanguide.org/storing-water-in-plastic-bottles/
Radios – This one page on our website gets by far the most readers!
https://emergencyplanguide.org/reviews/emergency-radio-reviews/
Walkie-talkies – Second most popular page on our website!
https://emergencyplanguide.org/reviews/walkie-talkie-reviews/
Miscellaneous specialty items
Trash compactor bags -
https://emergencyplanguide.org/managing-sewage-in-a-major-disaster/

Battery operated lanterns - https://emergencyplanguide.org/reviews/best-emergency-lanterns-for-power-outage/

Emergency generators - https://emergencyplanguide.org/portable-generator-safety-update/

COMMUNICATIONS WORKBOOK

If you are ready to set up your group communications network, get a copy of our free Communications Workbook. It's a companion to this book, and provides 15 more pages on what goes into setting up your teams and selecting the best procedures for communicating during an emergency. It is available for download at
https://emergencyplanguide.org/communications-workbook/

MEETING AGENDAS AND IDEAS

We've been holding neighborhood meetings for many years. We pulled together some of the best ones and have described each with a title, objective, procedure, materials needed and comments.

If you are in charge of training, you may find some inspiration here: Emergency Preparedness Meeting Ideas.

COMPANION WORKBOOK

Bring this book alive with the Emergency Preparedness for Mobilehome Communities WORKBOOK. Its question and answer format helps identify just what fits for your household or your community. Plenty of room for writing, highlighting and jotting down ideas.
https://emergencyplanguide.org/neighborh ood-disaster-survival-guide-series

OUR LATEST BOOKS

Emergency Preparedness Q&A Mini-Series – One topic each, covered via questions and answers. A quick read, easy to implement, perfect for getting started or for review. The collection of booklets can be used to put together a "course of study" for a household or a neighborhood group.

See details on all Mini-book titles at

https://EmergencyPlanGuide.org/Books

A few words more About the Author/s

As a team, Joe and I have worked with major corporations on disaster recovery programs and have headed up our neighborhood CERT team for a dozen years. Both of us are certified graduates of the FEMA CERT, NIM and ICS programs. In addition, Joe holds a General Class Amateur Radio Operator's license and is certified by the American Red Cross in Emergency Shelter Management. We continue to participate in monthly CERT update trainings offered by our city.

Joe won CERT Volunteer of the Year in 2007. And in 2015, our neighborhood group – with me at the helm --was awarded our city's First Annual Community Preparedness Award. A dozen of our team members have been recognized by our local police department for their response to emergencies.

We both do a lot of the work for our website and for our group, but I volunteered to put together this book. So it has MY name as author!

Virginia

Don't hesitate to write to us at https://emergencyplanguide.org/contact / with suggestions or questions. We'll share what we know and if possible, turn the conversation into an Advisory for our other readers.

A Last Legal Note – Can't be repeated too often

We have tried to make it clear that any group you assemble will be made up of volunteers. We think it's best to avoid the words "association" or "club" or "society" – anything that suggests official standing.

Why?

Careful wording in your recruiting, training and planning helps to protect you and your volunteers from any additional liability.

Volunteers trying to help out in an emergency can be expected to be protected by the Good Samaritan Laws of your state.

But the exact definition of who is covered by Good Samaritan Laws differs from state to state.

We encourage you to dig deeper about the Good Samaritan laws in YOUR state.

Next step: Please pass it along!

Our mantra: The more people who are prepared, the safer we all will be.

That's why we keep adding Advisories to our website each week, and why we committed to writing this book – hoping to reach out as widely as possible!

With that in mind, please help us get the word out by leaving a book review at Amazon. I'm sure you know that the more honest reviews, the more people are likely to look at, buy and use the book.

Here's how to leave a review:

- 48 hours after you have purchased the book, go back to Amazon.com. Go to *Books* and type in the name of this book: *Emergency Preparedness for Mobilehome Communities – Virginia S. Nicols*
- Scroll down past the product description to the Customer Reviews section.

- Click the box for Write a Review. You'll be presented with 5 gray stars. When you click on your choice, they'll turn gold and then you can write your review.
- Click "submit" when you've finished.

P.S. Amazon is looking for real reviews from real customers, so they won't publish your review unless you've spent at least $50 on Amazon within the past 12 months.

Amazon prompts you to include comments about what **other kinds of readers would benefit from the book**. What groups can you think of? While preparedness "family by family" is great, "group by group" would be even better for us all!

Thank you for reading, and for taking time to leave a detailed review at Amazon. You are important to spreading the word!

Made in United States
North Haven, CT
03 December 2022

27780243R00085